INTRODUCTION
SAY YES TO NO!

If you ever feel overwhelmed and overworked, or torn between competing pressures and unsure about which way to turn, there's a two-letter word you need to let into your life: NO.

When you activate the power of this word, you'll be able to lay down your own rules and set your own course. And you won't become a negative person: in fact, by saying no, you'll command respect from the people around you, and you'll have more mental space to focus on the things that matter to you.

We're going to start with a **Check-in**, to see how you're feeling about 'no' right now, and then we'll set about **Breaking the Taboo** surrounding it. We'll move on to look at **Setting Boundaries**, helping you to draw a line when you need to, and then we'll take a tour of **Every Kind of No**, exploring a wide range of situations where 'no' can help you achieve your aims. Finally, we'll look at solutions for some of the issues that arise **When No is Not Enough** before revisiting the check-in questions to see how you're going to activate 'no' in your life.

Each chapter is packed with information on the power of no, and there are lots of **No Labs** to give you practical advice on getting this word to work for you. In the **Stories of No**, we'll look at people who've used 'no' to make a difference, and in **Tune Out the Critics**, you'll find the ammunition you need to deal with any unhelpful pushback on your new wonder-word. So let's get started – it's time to unleash the power of NO!

CHECK-IN
BEFORE
WE
BEGIN...

Let's start by taking a look at where you are at the moment. Decide how true each of the statements in the table is for you, and tick the box that matches how you feel.

It's possible that even reading this list might make you feel a little uncomfortable: that's because dealing with problems is never the easiest thing to do. But the best way to tackle subjects that make us feel slightly off-balance is to face them openly. By the time we reach the end of the book, we'll be equipped to handle tricky situations more calmly, and to use the power of no for everyone's benefit.

I can say no to an invitation when I don't want to go to an event.

I can say no to my boss when I need to.

I can say no to salespeople when I don't want to buy something.

I can say no to friends and family when they ask me for something I don't want to give.

I can say no to my partner when I don't agree with them.

I can say no in a discussion without feeling afraid I'll start an argument.

I can say no when I want to stand up for what I believe in.

NEVER	NOT OFTEN	SOMETIMES	OFTEN	ALWAYS

BREAKING
THE
TABOO

Ouch! It's not nice when people say no to us. And although no is one of the first words we learn, it's one we're also trained to suppress throughout our upbringing. As we grow up, for many of us our natural inclination is to always say yes.

However, 'no' is a very powerful word. If we can overcome our unwillingness to use it, we'll discover that the world doesn't end when we say it – in fact, breaking the taboo around 'no' can help us live a more positive and successful life.

The word 'no' gets a bad rap, but saying no and being negative are actually two very different things. Negativity is a passive and enduring state. 'No', on the other hand, is an active choice in a specific moment: when you say it, you engage with the world, taking an empowered decision.

We say no because we have weighed up our options and decided that another course of action is right for us.

No, I won't sign your
petition because I
don't agree with what
you're campaigning for.

Thank you for inviting me,
but I already have other
commitments that take priority.

No, I won't have
another drink – I have
to work tomorrow.

Whether we state these reasons aloud or keep them
to ourselves, the act of choosing what's right for us is
powerful. Although we may be criticised for saying no,
making a considered choice marks us out as independent
people. And it is a vital tool in achieving our goals.

AVOIDING NO IS NOT A SOLUTION

Can you get through life without saying no? Possibly –
but you're unlikely to be very happy if you do. Avoiding
difficult conversations or other points of conflict doesn't
make them go away, and in some cases, pretending
nothing is wrong may actually make a bad situation
deteriorate. Learning to cope with the word 'no' will
help you in the long run, even if it's uncomfortable
when you start.

If you're in a situation where you have an inner 'no'
that you are unwilling to let out, try asking yourself
these questions:

Are you trying to keep the peace at the
moment, even though you know in your heart
there's a problem that needs addressing? For
example, maybe you're in a relationship that
you know isn't working, but you don't want to
cause your partner pain by ending it.

Will saying yes make demands on your time that you don't want to commit to? The resentment this could cause will be bad for you and those close to you.

Are you only saying yes because you feel under pressure, and you're afraid of the reaction a 'no' will get? Do you actually need more time to decide, before committing?

When you answer these questions honestly, you'll discover whether your knee-jerk 'yes' really needs to be a 'no'.

NO LAB

START WITH
A SMALL NO

Just as you wouldn't kick off your new mountain-climbing hobby by tackling Everest, you don't have to go for the biggest, scariest 'nos' as you begin your journey.

If you're unused to saying no, you can practise on the training slopes of low-risk situations, especially ones where you're unlikely to meet the other person again.

ON THE STREET: Hey you, the lady with the smile, you'd like to help orphaned puppies, wouldn't you?

IN A RESTAURANT: Would you like to super-size that?

ON THE PHONE: Hello, can I just ask you a few questions to see how much money we can save you?

ON YOUR DOORSTEP: Have you ever wondered about the meaning of life?

In each case, a simple 'No, thanks' or 'Not today' will get you through, and then you can forget about the conversation and any disruption to your day it caused. Keep your answers short and sweet, firm but polite.

WHERE NO BEGINS –
AND HOW IT GETS LOST

Learning the word 'no' is a key milestone in child development, and we all went through a phase around the age of two where we used it often enough to drive anyone but the most patient parent round the bend. However frustrating this period is to our loved ones, it's a vital stage in our lives: saying no is how we learn to assert our independence and individuality.

Throughout the rest of our childhood, we spend a lot of time learning to master our inner 'no'. There are lessons that must be sat through, toys that must be shared, presents that must be waited for. We realise that we can't always say no, especially if we want to get along with our friends and classmates.

But although this process of gradually mastering our impulses enables us to put aside instant reactions in favour of long-term goals, sometimes the effect of our upbringing is to tell us that all our 'nos' should be suppressed, and that getting along with the people around us is the most important thing in life. When that happens, we lose an important tool in our emotional toolkit. But we all have the innate ability to say no – we just need to learn to start using it again.

You can be a good
person with a kind
heart and still say no.

LORI DESCHENE

NO LAB

THE CONSTRUCTIVE NO

———

If you're worrying about a difficult 'no' conversation that you need to have with someone, one useful technique for getting your head in the right place is to focus on what you want to achieve.

Do you want the other person to change their behaviour? Are you worried that they are hurting someone else, or hurting themselves? Do you simply want them to be aware of a situation? If you ask yourself these questions before beginning a conversation, it will be easier for you to frame your concerns and express them in a way that is honest and non-confrontational.

For example, if a friend has not been treating you with enough care and respect, say 'I'm worried about the way our friendship has changed, and I'm hoping that if I share some of what I'm feeling we might be able to become closer again.' This will signal to your friend that your 'no' is coming with positive intentions.

Focusing on a positive goal with this technique will give you more confidence and help you to move situations forward in a constructive way.

BREAKING THE TABOO

A STORY OF NO
TARANA BURKE

Tarana Burke shot to international fame in October 2017, when a vast wave of sexual abuse testimonies broke across the internet, under the hashtag MeToo.

Up to that point, Tarana had been working as an activist on projects to raise awareness of sexual abuse, and in particular how it affected girls and women from marginalised communities. In 2006, she founded a movement called Me Too, to unite women who have suffered assault, to help them heal from their experiences and to disrupt the systems that allow abuse to continue unchecked.

When actor Alyssa Milano used the same term, #MeToo, on Twitter in 2017, thousands of women around the world stepped forward to talk about their experiences and gain strength from solidarity. This led to global interest in Tarana's work, which continues to focus on grassroots projects that say no to the shame and silence that all too often accompany abuse. The #MeToo movement shows that when our boundaries have been disrespected, we can rebuild and grow stronger by coming together as a group to support one another.

Me Too, in a lot
of ways, is about
agency. It's not
about giving up your
agency, it's about
claiming it.

TARANA BURKE

NO LAB

GETTING TO NO

When we're facing a big decision, one way to find a clear direction is to look at it in terms of Strengths, Weaknesses, Opportunities and Threats.

Strengths and Weaknesses are internal factors. So, your strength could be that you're thoughtful, and your weakness might be that you lose confidence in a stressful situation. Acknowledging a weakness helps you to prepare – by planning what you want to say, for example – and sets you up for a successful outcome.

Opportunities and Threats are external factors, describing outcomes of your 'no'. New possibilities may open up: these are your opportunities. At the same time, negative outcomes are possible too, such as hurting someone's feelings, and these would go in the threats section.

Looking at a potential 'no' decision in this way will help you see the tangled jumble of feelings that goes into a difficult choice in a more objective way.

STRENGTHS	WEAKNESSES
OPPORTUNITIES	THREATS

A STORY OF NO
AMY BAKER

Aspiring travel writer Amy Baker was working as an assistant editor at an organisation offering practical and cultural advice to people planning an overseas move, and every day her own wanderlust grew more intense.

When Amy told her friends and family that she'd like to chuck in her safe, steady job and explore South America alone for six months to fulfil her dream of becoming a travel writer, they gave her all the advice she ever could have wanted – and much more besides. All their warnings sounded like a horror film of repeated assaults, shootings and encounters with dangerous animals, not to mention the even worse prospect of never being able to get a proper job again.

However, Amy said no to all the fearmongering, set off on an adventure with plenty of thrills and spills, and wrote about it in a book called *Miss-Adventures*. Since coming home, she has established herself as a successful writer, events organiser and podcaster – proving that saying no can help you to get exactly where you need to be in life.

Much of what I was hearing was absolutely crazy, over-the-top advice... so I stubbornly decided not to listen to a word of it!

AMY BAKER

WHY DO WE FIND IT SO HARD TO SAY WHAT WE MEAN?

Finding it hard to say no isn't the only issue some of us face: it can be part of a broader hesitancy about expressing the full range of our emotions with honesty and openness. Most of us carry a certain amount of emotional baggage, often stemming from our early childhood experiences, and this affects the way we form attachments with other people. Psychologists frequently divide attachment styles into three broad definitions:

✗ **ANXIOUS:** An anxious attachment style is common in people whose early needs were met unpredictably. Anxious people may be so focused on being accepted by others that they deprioritise their own needs and lose confidence in their own choices. Instead of saying no clearly, they may find refuge in 'I don't mind – what would you prefer?', which ends up putting a lot of strain on a relationship.

✗ AVOIDANT: Avoidant people learned from an early age that others cannot be trusted and may hurt them. People with avoidant attachment styles are unwilling to risk being vulnerable in front of others, and learn to suppress their 'nos' instead of seeking help and support when they need it.

✗ SECURE: People with a secure attachment style are able to trust others and can express intimacy without feeling stressed or insecure. In a trusting relationship, both partners are able to say and receive the word 'no' without endangering their long-term connection. They respect each other's autonomy, and give each other the space they need to grow and thrive.

It isn't just our early years that influence us, but also the patterns of behaviour we pick up from other people throughout our lives, including friends and partners.

By analysing our own attachment style, we can approach conversations with more self-awareness. This will enable our transactions to be calmer and more productive, even when they're difficult and involve saying no.

IS SAYING NO HARDER FOR WOMEN?

In a word: yes. Although it can be hard for anyone of any gender to say no, women as a group face an extra challenge. Throughout childhood, girls are praised for playing nicely and getting on well with one another, while boys receive more praise for winning than for being kind and gentle. Girls who express strong opinions - including saying no - are often criticised for being bossy or stroppy, words that are rarely applied to boys.

When we become adults, the patterns we learned in childhood remain influential. Women often struggle to have their 'nos' heard and understood, facing problems such as being talked over in meetings and told they're getting emotional if they express any form of disagreement. In contrast, men who say no are often praised for being strong and 'taking no prisoners'.

For women, saying no carries the risk of being seen as overly negative; but if we're going to achieve our goals, *all* of us need to build up our strength and resilience, and bring our 'no' power into our daily lives.

My goal now is to ... only do
the things I love, and not say
yes when I don't mean it.

SANDRA BULLOCK

TUNE OUT
THE CRITICS

'I think it's best if we all just try to get along.'

Yes, getting along with each other is great, but if someone tells you to sacrifice your opinion in favour of general harmony, their own motivation is unlikely to be very positive. By staying calm and treating others with respect when you express disagreement, you'll come out of the conversation without ending or even damaging your relationships with the people around you.

'Let's have a bit more positivity, shall we?'

Sometimes saying no is actually the positive choice. If someone is proposing a course of action that is risky, poorly thought out, in bad taste, or just plain wrong, according to your understanding, then saying no is the best thing for you to do. It may result in a more positive outcome for everyone than if you'd gone along with the general consensus.

No legacy is so rich as honesty.

WILLIAM SHAKESPEARE

NO LAB

VISUALISE A
SUCCESSFUL NO

Prepare yourself for a successful 'no' by using this simple visualisation process.

1. Imagine yourself in a place where you feel happy and calm. It could be somewhere you know well or an imaginary landscape.

2. Take a few deep, calming breaths and clear your mind of other thoughts and worries.

3. Now think about the case you're going to make: go into some detail here and say your reasons out loud. By doing this, you will convince yourself, as well as practise stating your reasons calmly. You can write down ideas if it helps you to marshal your thoughts.

4. Sitting or standing with a straight back and your shoulders relaxed, picture yourself answering the other person's statements in an even, confident tone.

5. Finally, see yourself walking away from the conversation with the outcome you desired.

Picturing yourself playing an active, assured role before you begin a tricky conversation will help you come out of it knowing that you've kept calm and achieved your aims.

A STORY OF NO
JACINDA ARDERN

In October 2017, Jacinda Ardern, the Leader of New
Zealand's Labour Party, became the youngest female
prime minister of her country at the age of 37. In January
of the following year, she announced that she was
pregnant, and that apart from a six-week maternity-leave
period, she intended to carry out her duties as prime
minister during and after her pregnancy. When faced
with intrusive questions from a television interviewer
about the details of her baby's conception, Jacinda
calmly moved the conversation onwards, saying no to his
attempts to undermine her – and she continued to say no
through her actions to anyone who might have imagined
that being pregnant stops a woman from achieving her
other aims in life.

One particularly striking image from Jacinda's
pregnancy shows her striding through Buckingham Palace
on a state visit to the UK, wearing a full-length feathered
Māori cloak and looking confident and strong. The photo
became an instant meme: an illustration of a woman who
says no to limitations projected by others.

I am not the first
woman to multitask.
I am not the first
woman to work and
have a baby. There
are many women
who have done
this before.

JACINDA ARDERN

The oldest, shortest
words – 'yes' and 'no' –
are those which require
the most thought.

PYTHAGORAS

THE FINAL WORD
A TABOO THAT'S
WORTH BREAKING

There are no two ways about it: saying no can be tough, not just because we don't do it often enough, but also because others aren't used to hearing it from us. But it really is worth overcoming those self-policing instincts that want you to say yes and seek an easy, conflict-free life. By activating the word 'no' in your daily vocabulary you'll be able to make progress towards your own goals, and protect yourself from the limitations and demands other people would like to make on you.

2

SETTING BOUNDARIES

Unless you're a hermit in a cave or a castaway on a desert island, you live in a world where lots of different people are making demands on your energy. Our parents and children, teachers and employers, friends, lovers and spouses all require our time. By knowing where our own boundaries are, we can make it easier to balance these competing calls on our limited resources.

Saying no is vital because it gives you the space and time you need to achieve your own aims. For example:

You want some time and space to practise a favourite hobby.

You need to focus on your work so you can meet a deadline.

You'd like to go for a walk by yourself, so you have a chance to calm down from the stresses of the day.

When you give your time to activities like these, you make yourself unavailable for other people's requests. But it isn't selfish to look after yourself: by investing in your own happiness, you enable yourself to flourish. Once you get used to setting boundaries, it will become much easier, and you and the people you spend time with will come to understand each other better, and build a foundation of trust: they will learn that you really mean what you say.

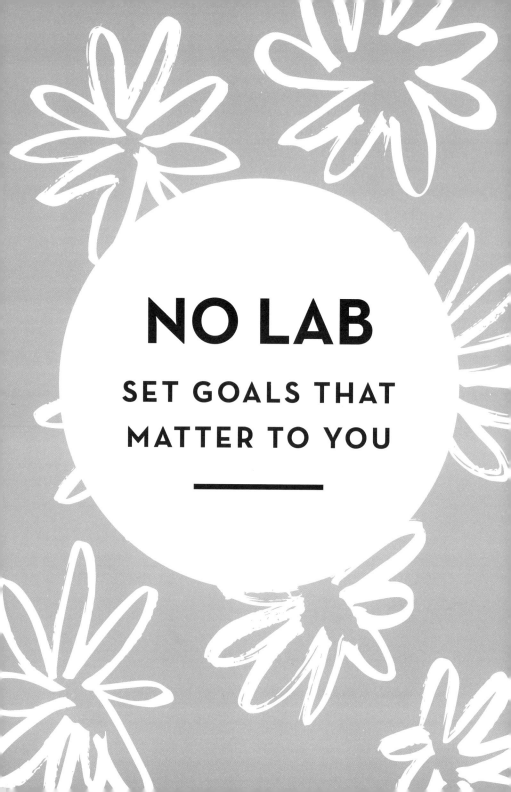

NO LAB

SET GOALS THAT MATTER TO YOU

———

Before we can start using our 'yeses' or 'nos' effectively, we need to know what's holding us back from getting what we actually want from life.

Sometimes in the daily round of work and family commitments, we can lose track of our personal priorities, so here's an exercise to help you refocus on your own ambitions. Take a notebook and write down headings for the main areas of your life, for example:

WORK   FRIENDSHIPS   HOBBIES

FAMILY   TRAVEL   RELATIONSHIPS

Now, ask yourself what would make each of these areas flourish. Make notes under each heading.

The next step is to look at the obstacles. These are the things you will need to say no to, in order to achieve happiness in each area. In this category, include self-limiting thoughts such as 'I'm not the kind of person who can do this'.

Finally, for each area, write down a statement about what you are going to change to get to where you'd like to be. Maybe you won't be able to achieve everything in one go ('give up my job and move to Spain'), but you can take some concrete steps to bring your dreams closer to reality ('start researching work options in Spain').

Give yourself permission to step out into a new identity, as a person who can do exciting things in new ways.

A STORY OF NO
JOHN BIRD

John Bird, now Baron Bird, had what anyone would call
a tough upbringing, becoming homeless at the age of five,
spending some years in an orphanage and then being
excluded from school. He had several spells in prison
during his teenage years and into his twenties, and he
used this time to learn to read, write and understand
the basics of printing.

In 1991, using his knowledge of publishing, John set up
a magazine called *The Big Issue*, with co-founder Gordon
Roddick. His aim was to provide people going through
homelessness and poverty with an opportunity to earn
an income for themselves: the magazine's slogan is
'a hand up, not a handout'. The self-employed vendors
buy copies of the magazine for half its cover price,
keeping the proceeds as their income. There is also a
Big Issue Foundation, which offers training and support
to vendors, helping them to rebuild their lives.

Since John Bird's initial decision to say no to our
inadequate response to homelessness, *The Big Issue*
has sold more than 200 million copies, and helped over
92,000 vendors in the UK. There are also nine other
international organisations under the 'Big Issue' umbrella,
in countries ranging from Australia to Zambia.

Optimism is something you have to fight for every day.

JOHN BIRD

NO LAB

PLOT YOUR
OWN COURSE

It's worth spending a little time in self-reflection, asking yourself how your new 'nos' fit in to the world around you. The answers will be different for everyone, and will depend on factors such as who else is involved and what your own personal goals are.

HOW DOES THE DECISION FIT WITH YOUR OWN PRINCIPLES AND VALUES? Perhaps you feel good about being known for your generosity, but then a friend asks you for something you're not morally comfortable with, such as lying to get them out of trouble. Saying no will make you value your own judgement, even if it puts pressure on your friendship in the short term.

WILL SAYING NO HELP YOU TO STAY ON TRACK WITH YOUR OWN GOALS? Just as airline attendants will tell you to see to your own oxygen mask before helping others with theirs, it's vital to keep your own goals in mind when deciding whether to say yes or no to other people.

WILL SAYING NO HELP YOU FIX A MISTAKE? One of the hardest types of 'no' happens when we are forced to admit that we're not on the right course. If you have a sinking feeling about your new job, your university course or your forthcoming wedding, and you know it's not just a blip, saying no to the status quo is essential for your happiness, even if it upsets the people around you at the time.

WHY WE RESIST SAYING NO

There are lots of motivations that can make us want to avoid saying no, for example:

We want other people to think we're 'nice'.

We don't want to cause pain.

We like to please people and make them happy at all times.

We don't like conflict.

Another reason we don't like to say no is that we know – from personal experience – how much it hurts. We are hardwired to hear 'no' more painfully than 'yes', and this means that while we can process pleasant events quickly and happily, negative events affect us more deeply and for longer.

However tough it is to say no, though, sometimes it's simply the right thing to do. Although it's not nice to see someone looking disappointed when we say no, that doesn't automatically make it the wrong choice. The alternative is that we disappoint ourselves, and if we keep doing that, we'll end up further and further away from our goals. In life, we can't always make everyone else happy – and that's OK.

NO LAB

SAY NO TO BEING A PEOPLE PLEASER

Does your face hurt from smiling and constantly saying yes through gritted teeth? If so, then you may have a serious case of people-pleasing-itis.

Never fear, though: this condition is fully treatable. The following steps will help you get your 'no' back.

1

TRY (LITERALLY) PLEASING YOURSELF: Although it sounds selfish, if you start by knowing what you really want, and what would make you happy, then when others make demands on you, it's easier to decide whether you really want to say yes or no.

2

GIVE YOURSELF BREATHING SPACE: It's tempting to say 'yes' immediately, but you don't have to. If you respond with 'Let me get back to you', you can check your schedule and work out whether you actually have time to commit.

LIMIT YOUR COMMITMENT: If you **3** don't state your boundaries, some people will blissfully assume you don't have any, unfortunately. By saying something like 'I can help at the barbecue, but I have to leave at 8pm', you're showing that you want to help, but your availability is limited.

4

DON'T OVER-EXPLAIN: You don't need to reel off a list of excuses when you say no – and in fact, the more reasons you give, the less convincing you are likely to sound. Remember that less is more.

5

ACCEPT THAT YOU CAN'T PLEASE EVERYONE: When you realise you don't need to make everyone happy, you will feel a huge sense of liberation. As the Rolling Stones sang, 'you can't always get what you want' – and when you apply this to the other people in your life and not just to yourself, you'll be able to say no with a clear conscience.

We must not confuse
the command to love
with the disease
to please.

———————

LYSA TERKEURST

NO LAB

THE POWER
OF BECAUSE

___

Not everyone will hear your 'no' or accept it as your final answer. One easy way of convincing other people to respect your boundaries is to give a reason.

Research has shown that using the word 'because' is a very simple and economic way of persuading someone and encouraging them to agree with you. It doesn't matter if the reason is untrue or not particularly strong – though you'll have less tricky footwork to do later if you're able to stick to the truth. By giving a reason, no matter how trivial, your refusal will be accepted more readily and the person will be more compliant.

In low-pressure situations, people tend to engage in automatic behaviour. If it's a relatively unimportant issue, you can give any reason at all and the other person will probably accept it. In a more important situation you may encounter greater resistance, but the magic word 'because' will help your 'no' gain traction.

No + because = YES!

AGGRESSIVE OR ASSERTIVE? FINDING THE RIGHT BALANCE

When conflicts arise in our relationships with other people, we have different options for how we react, relating to four basic communication styles.

PASSIVE: A passive communicator does not express their needs clearly, and is easily walked over by others. They are likely to accept another person's decision, but in doing so, may develop lingering feelings of resentment and anxiety.

AGGRESSIVE: In contrast, an aggressive communicator doesn't hesitate to state their needs, and will rarely pause before insisting that they get their own way. Although they may 'win' in the short term, their behaviour often springs from a deep-rooted insecurity.

PASSIVE-AGGRESSIVE:
A person with a passive-aggressive communication style doesn't lash out when a conflict occurs, but may find subtler ways of expressing their discontent, such as replying sarcastically or quietly undermining the other person.

ASSERTIVE: Finally, an assertive person is able to state their own needs clearly, and advocate for their point of view without causing pain to others. They can say yes or no as the occasion demands, without feeling that they have been bullied or that they have put unfair pressure on other people.

The people we tend to admire in our home and work environments, who manage to achieve their goals without leaving a trail of destruction, are those who have mastered the art of assertive communication.

NO LAB

ACTIVATE AN
ASSERTIVE NO

———

By learning to say no assertively, you will be able to protect your own boundaries without getting stressed, and you'll be equipped to deal with difficult conversations.

TRUST YOURSELF: Have faith in your right to say no: if you don't want to say yes, you don't have to.

PRACTISE: Running through a tricky conversation with a friend, or by yourself, will help you to prepare what you need to communicate.

DON'T APOLOGISE: By avoiding 'sorry' and 'I can't', you'll show that you won't be talked out of your 'no'.

USE OPEN BODY LANGUAGE: Sit in an upright position, with relaxed shoulders, and maintain eye contact.

SUGGEST AN ALTERNATIVE SOLUTION: If you can help in another way, make a suggestion – but don't feel obliged to if it's not possible.

A STORY OF NO
FREDRICK OUKO

In 1995, Fredrick Ouko, a Kenyan graduate with a diploma in business administration, went for a job interview. Despite being smartly dressed and having all the right qualifications for the post, his interview was over almost before it began. Fredrick realised this was because the interviewers were not prepared to see someone like him, who needed crutches or a wheelchair to get around, as a possible employee.

After several years of rejection based purely on his disability, Fredrick decided to tackle the problem of workplace discrimination head-on, and founded the Action Network for the Disabled in Kenya, known as ANDY. This organisation has two goals: to change negative perceptions held by employers about disabled people, and to empower those with disabilities.

By giving employers the information they need to help them see beyond their prejudices, Fredrick's organisation says no to discrimination in a positive and powerful way.

People just want to be given the same opportunities as their sisters and brothers.

FREDRICK OUKO

NO LAB

PROTECT YOUR
BOUNDARIES

———

Sometimes, no matter how well organised we are, life throws a curveball and all our planning goes out the window. We might be faced with an unexpected extra workload caused by a colleague's absence, an illness in the family or the break-up of a relationship. These tips will help you cope when your world feels out of control.

INCREASE YOUR SELF-CARE: It's precisely when you're under pressure that self-care is most important. Find time to look after *you*, even if it's only half an hour soaking in a bubble bath or strolling through the park.

USE YOUR NETWORK: Good friends will be more willing to pick up some of the strain than you might think. And support groups, both in person and online, are available to help you feel less alone.

LIMIT YOUR RESPONSIBILITIES: When you're under pressure, some of the people in your life will be blissfully unaware, and will ask things of you that they could do themselves. Focus on what *must* be done, and say no to tasks that others can handle. Once you start letting go, you'll be amazed at how many tasks fall into this category.

SWITCH OFF: Technology often makes it look as if we're available 24 hours a day – but we don't have to be. If you can't manage a whole day in one go, try a tech-free evening or even just an hour or two, and never take your phone to bed – it can sleep in another room!

TUNE OUT
THE CRITICS

'I want to show I can cope with anything.'

You are a brilliant person who's capable of doing a great many things, but nobody can do everything. We all have to factor in time for rest as well as doing all the tasks that we need and want to do. Be realistic about what you can and can't achieve, and where it's best to take a step back and ask for help.

> **'If you say no that easily, it shows you haven't got staying power.'**

This is one I've personally experienced, when I quit a job abroad that was making me utterly miserable. People who speak like this are projecting their own insecurities on to you, perhaps thinking of a time when they wish they had the strength to say no. Whatever their motivation, you don't have to take any notice. What matters is that you're making the right choice for you.

Boundaries are a part of self-care. They are healthy, normal, and necessary.

DOREEN VIRTUE

NO LAB

USE TEAM POWER TO MAKE YOUR NO HEARD

———

When you're in a situation where you feel that your voice is not being listened to, or you've experienced your 'no' being disrespected in the past, try bringing some friends on board. Here are some cases where team power can make a real difference.

IN THE DOCTOR'S OFFICE: If you feel nervous before a consultation, ask a friend to go with you. In the consulting room, they will give you confidence and help you articulate what you want to say – and say no if you need to. Alternatively, they can come with you to the waiting room to buoy you up before your appointment.

IN A DIFFICULT WORK CONVERSATION: If you know that a forthcoming meeting will be difficult, bring along a trusted colleague for moral support. It's best to discuss this with the meeting organiser first, and if it isn't possible, practise making your point beforehand with your colleague.

IN PUBLIC: If you are prepared to step in and support strangers when they say no, you're building a world where others will step in to help you, too. For example, if you see a woman on a bus being pestered by another passenger, you may be able to defuse the situation by striking up a conversation with her.

A STORY OF NO
LAURA BATES

After working as a research assistant, Laura Bates went on to find employment as an actor and nanny. She faced frequent sexism in her acting life, and she also found that the young girls she was caring for were worried about their body image. Her concern about these issues led her to found the Everyday Sexism website in 2012.

The website offers a simple form that anyone can fill in to share their experiences of sexism. There are no restrictions: stories can relate to home, work or any part of daily life, and no story is too small. The project's aim is to collect all kinds of experiences, particularly those that we tend to accept as normal because they're so common.

The project now runs in 25 countries and has over 280,000 followers on Twitter. By saying no to accepting and normalising experiences that others might describe as 'just having a laugh', Everyday Sexism has shown that when people come together in numbers, they cannot be ignored. Even if we're unable to say no at the moment when an event occurs, by sharing our stories we challenge behaviour patterns that should not be viewed as acceptable, and our combined testimony can lead to profound social change.

Stick together! The biggest success stories we hear from young women challenging sexism are from those who get together as a group and call it out.

LAURA BATES

YOU ARE NOT RESPONSIBLE FOR OTHER PEOPLE'S CHOICES

We've looked at situations that are frustrating or annoying – but there are of course other contexts where having your 'no' ignored can be deeply damaging, or dangerous.

If you are ever in a situation where someone transgresses your boundaries, asks you to do something inappropriate or makes you feel unsafe, you always have the right to say no. Sometimes we can't say anything, when fear makes us freeze, and if this happens you are never to blame. But if you can say no, do not be afraid to hurt the other person's feelings or cause public embarrassment. You do not have to tolerate abusive behaviour from anyone, whether it's a friend, partner, colleague or stranger. You have the right to say no to anything that makes you unhappy.

Saying no can
be the ultimate
self-care.

CLAUDIA BLACK

Daring to set boundaries
is about having the
courage to love ourselves,
even when we risk
disappointing others.

BRENÉ BROWN

THE FINAL WORD
IT'S OK TO ASK FOR HELP

When life throws up challenges, we often discover that we're stronger than we ever knew. Resources such as this book, advice websites and the support of your friends can take you a long way when things get tough and you need to deal with a conflict. However, if you feel that your boundaries have been transgressed and you're experiencing painful emotions, it may be a good idea to seek professional help.

Your doctor is there to listen to your problems, and can refer you to a specialist for further advice. There are also counsellors and therapists in the private and public sectors who are ready to listen to you and help you move forward.

3

EVERY KIND OF NO

Now that we've covered the value of protecting your own boundaries, it's time to put that theory into practice. This chapter focuses on lots of different types of 'no', and provides practical exercises that will help you to activate the power of this word exactly when and where you need it.

The Strength-Giving No

One of the sneakiest forms of negativity is the one that lives inside us, popping up to steal our self-confidence at the worst possible moment. If you catch yourself thinking 'I look awful today' or 'I'm not good enough', this is your inner saboteur chipping away at your self-esteem.

It's worth the struggle of saying no to this inner killjoy, because we have enough challenges in life without holding ourselves back, too. Self-esteem can be affected by lots of different issues, but we can give it a helping hand by being kind to ourselves and telling our inner critic to take an extended vacation.

NO LAB

SAY NO TO YOUR INNER CRITIC

———

It's not easy to break habits that may have been formed in childhood, but the benefits of pressing the mute button on your inner critic can't be underestimated.

RECOGNISE THE CRITIC: Tune in to the things your inner voice is saying to you, rather than just letting them slide into your consciousness. Our critical voice doesn't want to be spotted, but recognising it is the first step to making it go away.

EXPLORE HOW YOUR CRITICAL IMPULSE BEGAN: Perhaps you were bullied at school or your emotional needs were not met by your family. Understanding how your past affects your present is an important step in improving your future.

LOOK AT YOURSELF OBJECTIVELY: If you're used to listing your faults, consider whether these judgements make any sense from an outsider's view. Ask a friend for their opinion on the areas that seem faulty to you – their amazement will show how unfounded your fears are.

MAKE AN ACTION PLAN: Accept an invitation (because they do really like you), wear your swimsuit with pride (because you look great and nobody cares about your wobbly bits), or speak up at the company meeting (because your ideas are worth hearing). When you see that success leads to more success, you'll have even less time to spare for your inner critic's whisperings.

NO LAB

SAY NO TO FEAR
WITH A POWER POSE

———

In one of the most-watched TED talks of all time, social psychologist Amy Cuddy presented her theory that our posture has a powerful impact on our emotions.

Her research found that if people stood in an expansive pose before a mock-interview, they felt more confident than those who held a slouched position. The next time you have a stressful situation coming up, for example a job interview or a presentation, find a place where you can be alone and try one of the following positions.

✗ Lean back in a chair with your hands clasped behind your head and your feet up on a table.

✗ Stand with your feet more than hip-width apart, hands on hips (the 'Wonder Woman').

✗ Lean back in your chair, knees apart, with one arm draped casually over the chair next to you.

✗ Stand at a desk, leaning forward with your hands planted firmly on the desktop.

✗ Stand like a giant starfish, with your feet far apart and your hands reaching up to opposite corners of the room.

Hold this position for two minutes. You should find that you feel more empowered as a result of the exercise.

A STORY OF NO
SOFIE HAGEN

Danish comedian Sofie Hagen has gained a loyal following
for her honesty and wit – she now has tens of thousands
of followers on social media, and draws packed houses
for her stand-up shows.

For her comedy, Sofie digs deep into her experiences,
finding unexpected humour in subjects such as her
anxiety, the abuse she suffered in childhood and her
relationship with her body, and she is uncompromising
about her right to be exactly who she is. As an outspoken
figure in the body-positivity movement, Sofie says no to
the quest for a so-called 'perfect' body. She refuses to
be shamed into silence about her own issues, and in her
Made of Human podcast she celebrates diversity in all its
forms, and also features a regular 'act of disobedience',
where her listeners describe times they've stood up
against society's oppressions.

Sofie is continuing her campaign to say no to toxic
body standards in a new book. Her story proves that
when we refuse to listen to our inner critic, we can have
much more joy in our lives, and make an impact on the
world around us.

If you want to be truly healthy, stop thinking in kilos and circumference. Think about what will nurture your body – and mind.

SOFIE HAGEN

The Self-Control No

Compared to any previous generation, we have many more opportunities to be distracted and entertained. Our phones ping with instant messages and 'likes', and our TVs and computers allow us to binge on endless hours of comedy and drama. As a result, we can feel that our attention is constantly expended, and that it's hard to get anything done that requires deep concentration.

In order to achieve our full potential, we need to learn to say no to self-indulgence and bingeing: it's as important to set boundaries for ourselves as it is for other people. By putting some good habits in place, we can resist the lure of constant entertainment and achieve goals that are important to us.

NO LAB

PRACTISE IMPULSE
CONTROL

Underneath our rational thought processes lies a noisier part of our consciousness, the part that wants everything right now and doesn't understand the concept of delayed gratification.

Although we all experience this conflict, with practice we can learn to control our impulses.

LISTEN TO YOUR INNER VOICE: Ask yourself what is really important to you. Most of us have things we want to achieve that require time and commitment, such as writing a book, training for a marathon, learning a language or passing an exam. If you have a clearly defined long-term goal, you'll have a reason to overcome your quick-win impulse in favour of a step towards your bigger achievement.

MEASURE YOUR SCREEN TIME: If you find your online life often takes up too much of your free time, download an app to measure exactly how many hours per day you are spending glued to your devices. You may be shocked at first, but seeing your stats will motivate you to bring those red numbers down into the safe green zone again.

FIND PRACTICAL SHORTCUTS TO HELP YOU:
You'll find it much easier to avoid distraction if you place the objects of temptation out of sight, either in a bag or another room. Another strategy is to allow yourself time online only at specific points in the day or in certain places. A friend of mine keeps her smartphone in the kitchen near the kettle: whenever she's making a cup of tea, she allows herself a Twitter splurge, but anywhere else, phone-browsing is out of bounds.

GET A BUDDY ON BOARD WITH YOU: If you are finding it hard to stay focused, use accountability to help you stick to your promises. We don't like letting other people down, so tell a friend what you're working on, and give them regular progress updates, such as 'I worked on my short story for two hours today'. Getting your goals out in the open like this can help you stick with them when temptations beckon.

Learning to control your 'I want it now' impulses will bring other positive side-effects, as well as helping you to focus on your long-term goals. For example, by taking control of your screen time, you are likely to sleep better and see an overall improvement in your ability to concentrate. You really have nothing to lose.

Focusing is about
saying no.

STEVE JOBS

No
Among
Friends

Good friends enjoy being together, they're generous with their time and resources, and their default position is likely to be 'yes' – because friendship is a kind of 'yes' in itself. However, from time to time we have to say no even to our best friends, because none of us has a bottomless reserve to give from.

One of the hard things about saying no is that, however kindly we say it, the other person may still react emotionally, because 'no' always stings, and when someone isn't expecting it the sting is all the harder. But you're not responsible for your friend's emotions: if you need to say no to maintain your boundaries, that's OK. A good friendship will survive and even thrive when you communicate truthfully about your needs.

NO LAB

AN INOFFENSIVE NO

When a friend asks you for something that you can't or don't want to do, don't panic. Just be honest about your reasons as kindly as possible, and don't feel you need to over-explain.

✗ If a friend wants to tell you all their problems but you're exhausted after a long day: 'I'm sorry, I'm really tired right now and I can't give you my best attention. Can I call you tomorrow instead?' If you give an alternative, make sure you stay true to your offer.

✗ If a friend asks you to go on an expensive night out that you can't afford: 'I'm sorry, I don't have the budget for that – let's go on a picnic together instead.' Offering a different plan shows you care about the friendship. Don't allow peer pressure ('But everyone else is coming') to sway you if you know it's not right for you.

✗ A little white lie can help if you really want to say 'No way!' but don't want to offend. For example, if a friend asks to borrow your make-up brushes or lip balm: 'I'm sorry, I have a cold coming on and I'd hate you to get it.'

✗ If being polite and gentle doesn't work, a simple 'I'm sorry, I can't' will do the trick.

The
Dating
No

Women in particular are given messages throughout their lives that love and sexual satisfaction will come to them if they try hard to look their best, or if they show that they're not threatening. The problem with this kind of programming is that it can lead us to become disconnected from our authentic impulses to say yes and no. We end up compromising too much, and then when we get into bed, we feel frustrated if our partner doesn't know how to please us.

To make the most out of saying yes or even 'yes yes YES!' in a romantic situation, it helps if we feel empowered to say no. Wherever your 'nos' fall, you have a right to express them – and a good partner will be willing to listen. If a partner doesn't treat you the way you deserve, then that behaviour merits a 'no' as well.

NO LAB

SAY NO TO
NEGGING

———

Ugh, we've all been there: talking to someone at a party and realising that they are using subtle (or not-so-subtle) insults to bring us down.

Today it's called negging, and it could be a backhanded compliment, a culturally offensive comment, an unsolicited critical suggestion or any other remark intended to wrongfoot the recipient. This strategy works because so many of us have been socialised to accept attention of any kind as a compliment. We all deserve better than this. Here's my negging shut-down kit.

1. Recognise that negging is designed to undermine your confidence. There's no place for this kind of behaviour in a respectful, non-toxic relationship, and identifying it is the first step to making it stop.

2. Look out for the danger signs that the person isn't treating you as an equal. Nobody is perfect but watch out for these clues: turning up late and not apologising, being rude to waiting staff, looking at their phone while you're talking to them, ignoring what you say or constantly interrupting you to tell you their 'better' opinion.

3. Shut it down, using one of the following strategies. Always keep yourself safe, especially in a face-to-face situation.

Hit the other person right back with a comeback remark or insult – and not in a flirty way. Make it clear you're not joking.

Call them out for what they're trying: 'Oh yeah, negging – so original. Marks out of ten? Zero.'

If words fail you, you can always just leave. You don't have to be polite, and leaving is another way of saying no.

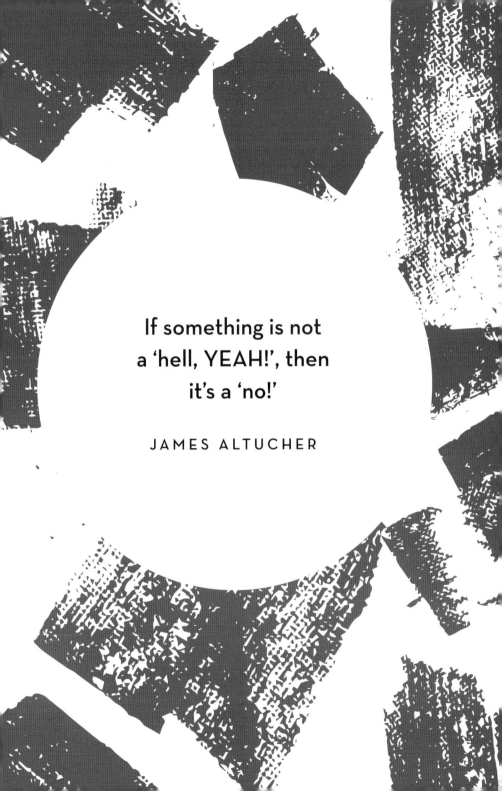

If something is not
a 'hell, YEAH!', then
it's a 'no!'

JAMES ALTUCHER

NO LAB

SAY NO TO GASLIGHTING

———

Have you ever been in a relationship where your partner regularly made you doubt your own perceptions? This practice, known as gaslighting, is about maintaining power over someone. Here are some typical signs.

✗ The other person behaves inconsistently, for example, by saying they love horror movies but rejecting the horror-film boxset you buy them for Christmas.

✗ The other person flies into an angry rage, then forgives *you* for whatever set them off in the first place.

✗ The other person makes you doubt your abilities: 'That's not bad, considering you're not much of a cook.'

✗ The other person makes light of your emotions: 'Oh come on, it was only a joke – stop being so sensitive!'

The first step in saying no to gaslighting is to **recognise** that it's happening. Next, it's good to **discuss** the problem with a trusted friend or counsellor – their view will help you to clarify exactly what's happening. Finally, you need to **decide** whether to continue the relationship.

If it's a work situation, you may be able to reduce your exposure to the gaslighter. In a personal relationship, counselling may be a positive next step, though if the other person has fallen into a pattern of manipulating you, it's likely that giving yourself some distance from them will make you feel happier.

The Professional No

Our jobs keep us busy; they give us satisfaction, at least sometimes, and help us pay the rent. But on top of all these marvellous qualities, work is also a major source of stress. There are too many emails to answer, too many competing responsibilities to juggle, and when you add workplace politics into the mix, things can get overwhelming. This is where 'no' is your friend. However difficult it may feel, if you can use 'no' at work, you'll be more effective and able to progress in your career.

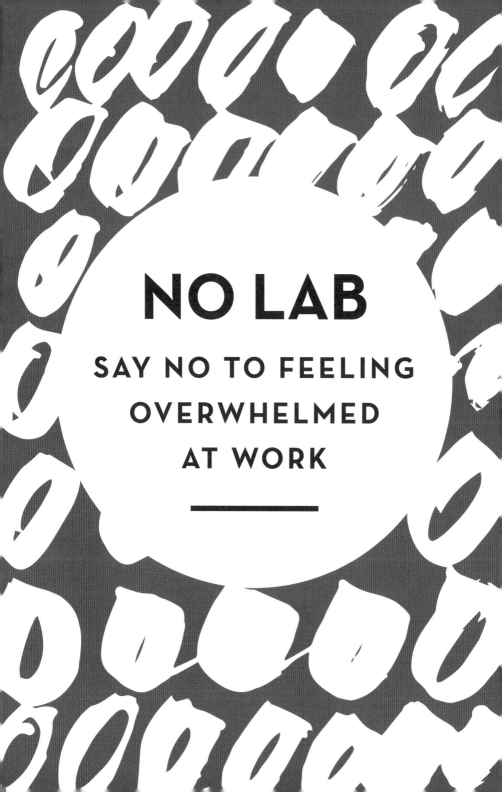

NO LAB

SAY NO TO FEELING
OVERWHELMED
AT WORK

———

'Too much to do!' is a cry that goes up from workplaces all across the land, every day. Use these techniques to see off crises before they reach your desk.

SET 'SMART' GOALS: If your manager gives you a fluffy target, such as 'make the department run better', work with them to establish exactly what they're looking for. SMART goals are Specific, Measurable, Achievable, Relevant and Time-bound. By applying these criteria to the important tasks you have to fulfil, it'll be clear to you and your employer how successful you are.

BREAK BIG TASKS INTO SMALL STEPS: If you're given a big project, break it into manageable chunks. Not only is each smaller task easier to get done, but you may also be able to delegate them, and track progress without constantly having to look at the entire project as a whole.

COMMUNICATE: If your workload is too big, talk to your manager. They may not be thrilled to hear that everything can't be done right away, but they will be grateful for your honesty: it'll be worse if the deadline passes and the work hasn't been finished. Equally, if your manager tries to give you extra work when you're already at full capacity, use questions such as 'I won't have time to finish my current jobs if I take this on as well: which one are you happy to wait longer for?' Your manager is then obliged to take responsibility for the changed workload.

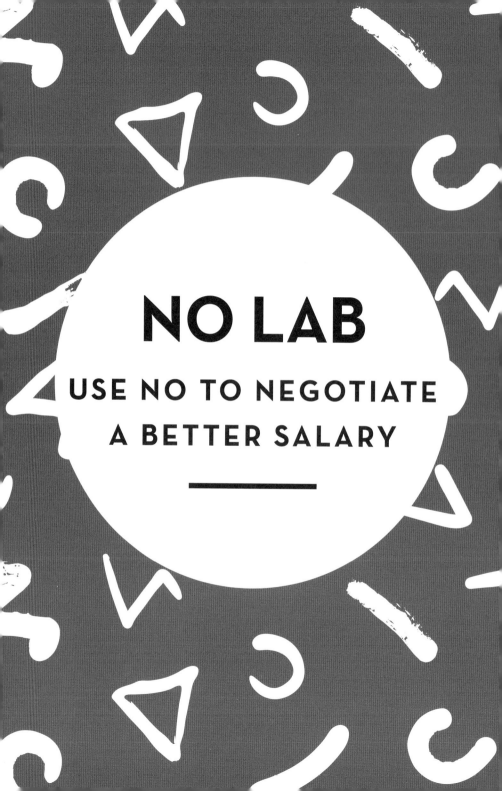

NO LAB

USE NO TO NEGOTIATE A BETTER SALARY

———

Meetings about our salaries can be awkward, because we're taught from an early age that discussing money is vulgar, and we often feel that all the power rests with our employer. By coming to the negotiation table with a strong 'no' game, you'll be able to get the best outcome. Follow the pathway below to find the right result for you.

PREPARATION IS KEY: Before you enter the meeting room, prepare the evidence you'll need to support your case. How does your desired rate of pay match similar posts across the company or the wider industry? What have you achieved so far in your career that demonstrates your financial worth?

DECIDE WHAT YOU'RE WILLING TO OFFER OR CONCEDE: Are you prepared to take on extra responsibilities or learn a new skill? If you don't get what you've asked for, what level would be acceptable to you?

SWITCH OFF YOUR INNATE DESIRE TO MAKE OTHER PEOPLE HAPPY: You can aim for a win–win outcome, but your primary consideration has to be achieving your goals. Remember, your manager may play on your desire to please: be polite but don't fall into this trap.

SILENCE CAN BE ANOTHER FORM OF 'NO': Don't feel you have to fill every gap in the conversation. Just a little bit of uncomfortable silence can encourage the other person to offer concessions.

If you didn't get what you want, but you don't want to slam the door, say 'I understand your position but I'd like to organise a salary review meeting in six months' time', or 'I realise that's your best offer for now, and I need time to consider it'.

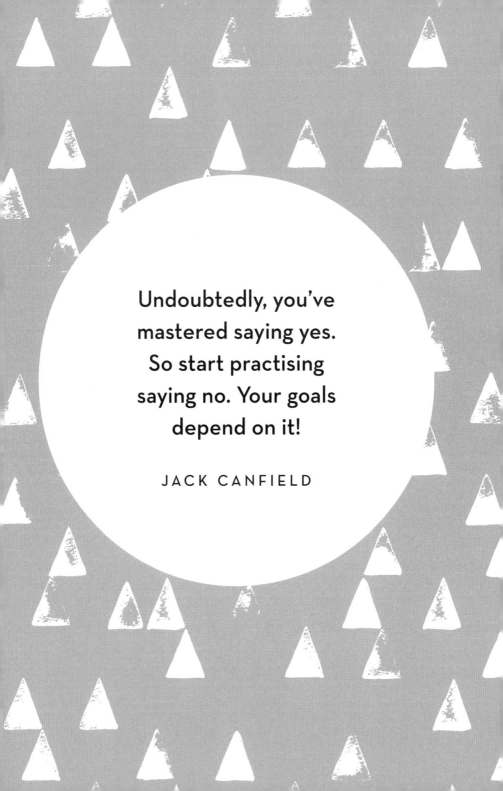

Undoubtedly, you've mastered saying yes. So start practising saying no. Your goals depend on it!

JACK CANFIELD

A STORY OF NO
THE WOMEN OF ICELAND

Pay inequality between men and women is an issue that continues to afflict the world today, and it's thanks to the tireless work of campaigners that we are made aware of it.

Among the pioneers of the campaign for pay equality are the women of Iceland, who on 24 October, 1975 staged a national 'women's day off' to protest the fact that women were earning on average only 60 percent of men's wages. Ninety percent of the female population of the country participated, refusing to go to work or carry out domestic tasks. As a result, no newspapers were printed, the telephone service was shut down and many schools and factories closed for the day.

By saying no to their normal work for just one day, Iceland's women demonstrated how much the country relies on and undervalues them. Their action led to changes in the law to improve equality but the battle is not yet won, and the women of Iceland still protest by leaving work early in certain years on 24 October, at a time of day chosen to reflect the exact gap between men's and women's pay. Their continuing refusal to accept the status quo means that employers throughout the country cannot ignore the issue.

There was a
tremendous power
in it all and a great
feeling of solidarity
and strength among all
those women standing
on the square in
the sunshine.

VIGDÍS FINNBOGADÓTTIR

The
Public
No

If something isn't going the way you want it to in your home or work life, it's usually possible to make a difference in some way: you can talk it through with someone or make an immediate change to improve things. But when we start looking at the wider community, whether it's our town, our country or the world, there are problems that are far too huge for us to grapple with as individuals.

One response to feeling powerless is to curl up under a blanket and hide, but avoiding the problems in the world around us won't make them go away, and being able to ignore them is a luxury that many others don't have.

When we join together with like-minded people, we can use the power of no to go out into the world and start making a real difference.

NO LAB

BUILD A NO THAT CAN'T BE IGNORED

———

If you see an injustice and want to do something about it, take your 'no' into the public domain and make sure you are heard. When you persist and work with other people, you'll be amazed at how much impact you can make.

BE AWARE OF THE BIGGER PICTURE: Instead of following the same routines, think about what is happening in your area. Are the roads safe enough? Is public transport affordable? Is your community well looked after by its politicians? When you start to think analytically about the world around you – both locally and farther afield – then you can start to bring about positive change.

ONLINE CAMPAIGNING: It's not just time-wasting or grandstanding; when enough people protest on social media, companies and governments take action. If you think an organisation is behaving in an unprincipled way, saying no to their actions on a public forum is a very effective way of encouraging them to change.

GROUP PROTESTS: One voice may be small, but thousands of voices together are impossible to ignore. For the great issues of our time, there are regular demonstrations, which are well organised and legal. If you have a 'no' that needs expressing, adding your voice to a larger group is a perfect way to make your protest heard.

A STORY OF NO
THE PEOPLE OF ESTONIA

Choral singing has long been a tradition in Estonian culture, and through invasions and occupations over the centuries, coming together to sing has been a vital way for Estonian people to express their national identity.

During the Second World War, the Soviet Union annexed Estonia and, despite promising to honour the nation's sovereignty, took over its government, killing or deporting its leaders. The following decades saw a process of 'Russification', under which Russian language and culture were made the norms. Throughout the Soviet era, music was a key form of Estonian resistance. In 1969, for example, a crowd of over 100,000 sang the national song 'Land of My Father, Land That I Love' and ignored demands for them to stop, even drowning out a military band that was trying to disrupt them.

In the late 1980s, the Estonian people expressed their desire for change through a 'Singing Revolution'. Between 1987 and 1991, crowds would gather to sing patriotic songs in acts of peaceful defiance, leading eventually to the nation's independence on 22 August, 1991. These large-scale gatherings were impossible for the authorities to ignore and represented a very powerful and unusual way to say no to a system that refused to listen.

A nation who makes its revolution by singing and smiling should be a sublime example to all.

HEINZ VALK

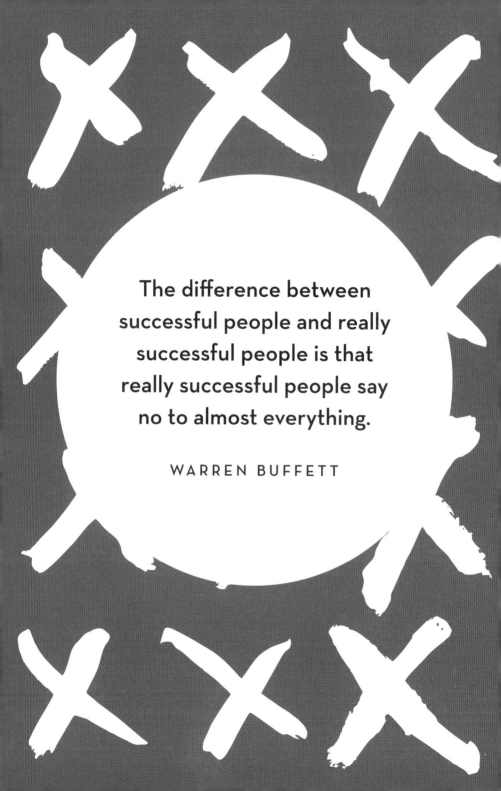

The difference between successful people and really successful people is that really successful people say no to almost everything.

WARREN BUFFETT

THE FINAL WORD
CELEBRATE YOUR VICTORIES

There are countless places and contexts where a 'no' can help get you closer to where you need to be, whether it's at work, at home or in the wider world. Learning to become confident with your 'nos' takes time and practice, and you may find that sometimes your efforts don't result in exactly the outcome you wanted. This remains true even for skilled users of the power of no, because life doesn't always give us what we want. So, keep your 'nos' ready, stay adaptable, and celebrate each victory as it comes.

WHEN NO IS NOT ENOUGH

We've looked at techniques for maximising your 'no'-power, and you're now ready to go out into the world with a 'no' that's as strong as your 'yes'. No matter how well-equipped you are with the power of no, sometimes people won't hear you. So now it's time to decide how to cope when 'no' is not enough.

NO LAB

THINK ABOUT YOUR WALK-AWAY POINT

———

In many cases, you may be able to live with the outcome if you didn't get the result you wanted when explaining your needs, disucussing a problem or negotiating a deal, and you can try again another time.

However, if you're unhappy with the way your 'no' has been received, your most positive choice may be to remove yourself from that situation – you could decide to find another job or not to go to that social event. You'll be best prepared to do this if you've taken time to think deeply about what matters to you, and especially if you've already tried to improve things. Nobody wants to be a giver-upper – but sometimes walking away is the right choice, for your health and well-being.

If you do walk away, draw a line under the situation and move on with as little ill-will as possible. When you focus on the future, and make the best of the situation you're in now, you will be happier than if you ruminate on the conflict.

NO LAB

HOW TO DEAL
WITH HARD
CONVERSATIONS

———

It often seems easier to ignore problems that spring up between us and our colleagues, friends and family members, but in the long run, avoidance can make things worse, so it's worth overcoming our fears and facing our problems together. Follow these tips to make tricky conversations easier.

PREPARE YOURSELF: Before the conversation, gather your thoughts about what hasn't been going right, and how you propose it could be changed for the better.

FIND A GOOD TIME AND PLACE: It's best to let the other person know in advance that you want to discuss something sensitive with them, so it doesn't come as a surprise. A quiet, private space is likely to be more suitable than a busy, public one such as a crowded café.

BEGIN WITH A POSITIVE: Start by expressing something you like about your relationship, so the other person understands that the reason you're going in deep right now is because you want the connection between you to grow even stronger.

STAY FACTUAL AND SPECIFIC: This is not the time to say 'You're always late' or 'You never call me'. Talk about particular moments that upset you, rather than painting a broad-brush picture.

USE 'I...' STATEMENTS: Putting yourself first is actually really helpful in difficult conversations. 'I felt embarrassed when you laughed at me in front of the others' is more constructive and less likely to provoke a defensive reaction than 'You embarrassed me in front of the others'.

BE RESPECTFUL: If you feel your emotional temperature rising, take a deep breath to calm yourself down, or even take a short break from the conversation if you need to. Insulting the other person or raising your voice will put the other person on the attack and won't help you resolve the issue.

ASK OPEN QUESTIONS: You'll achieve more insight into the other person's state of mind if you ask questions starting with *how, why, where* and *when* instead of closed questions that only require a yes or no answer.

LOOK FOR A POSITIVE OUTCOME: When it's time to bring the conversation to a close, try to find common ground and a way forward. Even if the two of you haven't managed to solve the problem, you will have gained more understanding of each other. Try to find a next step, such as another meeting or an agreement to call each other, so you both know that the connection between you will keep going.

Our opinions and thoughts mean very little if there is nothing we disagree with.

HENRY CLOUD

NO LAB

HOW TO MAKE A GOOD APOLOGY

———

Saying sorry is perhaps even harder than saying no – but it's worth doing it well. There's not much that's more frustrating than receiving a half-baked apology, and it definitely doesn't set a relationship up for success in the future.

If you want to receive decent apologies, it helps to know how to give one when the need arises, so here are my tips for apologising effectively. By using these strategies, you'll also know when you've been offered the real thing when it's your turn to receive an apology.

BE SPECIFIC: You don't need to make blanket condemnations about yourself ('I'm so stupid', 'I don't know what's wrong with me', 'I'm not good enough for this job'). Stay focused on the issue itself, and trust that you are actually good at what you do – you're just a normal person who occasionally makes mistakes.

BE GENUINE: It's easy to feel defensive when you're in the wrong, but if you find yourself reaching automatically for excuses ('It's not my fault', 'You should have told me', 'How could I have known') without examining whether you're really at fault, take a moment to ask yourself whether your reaction bears comparison to the facts of the matter.

EMPATHISE: Think about how the issue has affected the other person, and imagine how you'd feel if it happened to you. What may seem trivial to you ('The gift was only delivered a day late') might have had a significant impact on someone else ('It arrived too late for my mother's birthday party').

TAKE STEPS TO AVOID THE PROBLEM IN FUTURE: Whether the other person knows about this or not, making a plan to stop this mistake happening again will benefit you and your contacts. You may need help from a manager if the problem was related to work overload or time management, but you might be able to implement useful changes by yourself. So for example, if you missed an important deadline, perhaps you need to review your schedule or ask for help because you're overloaded; if you overslept and got to work late again, you could try going to bed earlier or replacing your alarm clock.

The best way out
is always through.

ROBERT FROST

NO LAB

SAY NO TO OVER-APOLOGISING

———

When you accept that everyone makes mistakes, you'll be able to cope better when they happen.

REMEMBER YOU'RE NOT ALONE: Remind yourself of funny stories you've heard about screw-ups your friends and colleagues have made, whether it was printing a book with a typo on the cover (yes, that was me, and I'm almost over it) or saying something embarrassing in public (this happens to all of us at some point).

TAKE A LONGER PERSPECTIVE: It's hard to imagine now, but that mistake that's making your stomach clench right now won't feel nearly as bad in a week's time. In a month's time it'll hurt less and in a year's time you may have trouble even remembering what happened.

DON'T LET THE ISSUE CLOUD YOUR FREE TIME: If you've apologised and done whatever you can to solve the problem, that's enough. Once you've hashed the mistake out, in your head or with a housemate or partner, make the decision to let it go.

SEE IT AS AN OPPORTUNITY FOR GROWTH: Every mistake has something to teach us. What are you going to take from this into the future? Find something positive – even if it's only 'I really screwed that up and look, I'm still here!' – then the mistake won't have been an entirely negative experience.

WHEN SAYING NO PUTS RELATIONSHIPS TO THE TEST

- -

Despite all the techniques for saying no carefully and thoughtfully, and despite thinking out your reasons with honesty and openness, you will find that some people are unable to accept your 'no' without a defensive reaction. When this happens in relationships, it can be painful. If you find you're in a relationship where the other person always makes demands of you, but refuses to pay attention when you set your own limits, it's possible your connection is based more on exploitation than respect.

When you realise this, you can take steps to address the situation, such as talking about the problems calmly and looking for a way forward. But in the end, if the other person still won't listen to you when you say no, you may be better off withdrawing from that connection, and focusing your time and love on people who respect you as much for your 'nos' as for your 'yeses'.

Anybody who gets upset
or expects you to say
yes all the time clearly
doesn't have your best
interest at heart.

STEPHANIE LAHART

NO LAB

SAY NO TO TOXIC FRIENDSHIPS

———

A good friendship is one where you trust each other, where being together lifts you both up. Toxic friendships, on the other hand, are ones where you feel worse when you're together.

You may be experiencing a toxic friendship if you regularly feel these things:

✖ The other person always offloads all their problems on to you, and doesn't ask about yours.

✖ You feel anxious before meeting the other person.

✖ You find yourself having to apologise a lot.

✖ The other person reinforces your feelings of self-doubt, and they don't celebrate your successes.

✖ Whatever happens to you, they always talk about how it affects *them*.

If you value the relationship, it's worth discussing your concerns with your friend: they may be shocked to realise their behaviour is bringing you down. If this approach doesn't work, you could choose to spend more time with other friends and become less available to this person. Finally, if things are beyond repair, your best choice may be to cut them out of your life. It's never easy doing this, but looking after your own well-being is so important that it may be the right choice for you.

TUNE OUT
THE CRITICS

*'I'm sorry if your feelings
are hurt but you're taking
this too seriously.'*

We've all heard this, right? It is the ultimate non-apology: the speaker is using the magic word 'sorry', but in a way that avoids taking any responsibility for what has happened, and instead places the blame on you for being over-emotional. If someone says this to you, you can repeat what actually happened and why it matters, or you may choose to let this person have as little involvement in your life as possible.

'You'll break his/her heart if you walk away from this relationship.'

If life inside your relationship is crushing your soul, then protecting your partner's feelings can't be your first priority. Friends and family often want the fairy tale to be real, but they don't know what it feels like from the inside. If you know it's time to go, trust your gut and accept that not everyone will understand your decision. The ones who matter will support you.

It is necessary, and even vital, to set standards for your life and the people you allow in it.

MANDY HALE

NO LAB

SAY NO TO LIVING
A SMALL LIFE

At home and at work, we're constantly balancing our inner desires against the needs and expectations of other people. This can be draining, especially if we continually put our own wishes on the back burner, and one day we may find ourselves wondering why we didn't take more opportunities to be happy when we had the chance. These habits that will help you live the bigger, happier life that you deserve.

BE A PERSON WHO MAKES THINGS HAPPEN: It's nice to be asked on a date, to a party, to an important meeting – but if you always wait to be asked, you'll miss lots of opportunities to grow. Putting yourself forward can be embarrassing if the other person says no, but if you never take any chances, you will regret your caution later.

ACCEPT THAT CONFRONTATION IS SOMETIMES NECESSARY: Talking things through can help clear the air, and sometimes even makes things much better than before. Brace yourself and don't shy away from the tricky conversations you know you need to have.

WHEN NO IS NOT ENOUGH

STAY IN TOUCH WITH YOUR DREAMS: It's easy to make grand plans when we're on holiday or newly in love, but much harder when we're on a crowded bus on a rainy Monday morning, with a staff meeting lying ahead of us. By checking in with your life goals regularly, you'll be able to see how well your current lifestyle is helping you get where you want to be – and you'll be able to make changes if you need to.

EXPRESS YOURSELF: This is the simplest, most important and somehow also the most challenging way to say no to a small life. You have emotions, desires, dreams, reactions and opinions, and you deserve the time and space to let these flower. Try to spend as much time as you can with people who appreciate what makes you *you* – because people who accept and love us for our authentic selves are the ones to treasure in life.

It's only by saying no that you can concentrate on the things that really matter.

SCOTT BELSKY

A STORY OF NO
BILL AND MELINDA GATES

In 1997, Bill Gates, the principal founder of Microsoft, and his wife, Melinda, read an article about the millions of children around the world who die from diseases carried by their drinking water – diseases that had long since been eradicated in the USA. This sowed the seed of an idea which came to fruition in 2000 as the Bill and Melinda Gates Foundation, a non-profit organisation dedicated to reducing poverty and improving healthcare around the world.

Their goals include the elimination of polio and malaria, and the control of the spread of HIV and tuberculosis. Even for one of the richest people in the world, the idea of saying no to the world's most widespread diseases seems ambitious, if not impossible. But in 2014, partly as a result of support from the Gates Foundation, the World Health Organisation declared India to be officially free of polio, a status which continues to this day. And through their work in over 100 countries, the Foundation continues to make a difference to countless lives.

Once you've taken care of yourself and your children, the best use of extra wealth is to give it back to society.

BILL GATES

When you say yes
to others, make sure
you are not saying no
to yourself.

PAULO COELHO

THE FINAL WORD
TRUST YOURSELF AND KEEP FAITH IN YOUR POWER OF NO

It's challenging to learn how to use 'no' effectively, and you won't always do it perfectly. If you're too forceful, it's OK to apologise, learn from the experience and move on with a clean slate. If you change your mind about something you said no to, nobody can force you to stick to each decision forever. Finally, sometimes no matter how well you use your 'no', the other person won't respect it. This is frustrating, and even in a close relationship your best choice may be to walk away. It's painful when this happens, but you have the right to be safe and happy, and to do what's best for you.

CONCLUSION

EMBRACING THE POWER OF NO

———

We've taken a rollercoaster ride through many areas of our lives where the word 'no' can help us to live a life that's truly fulfilling.
If you focus on the themes that matter most to you, you'll be able to find opportunities to make things better with this powerful two-letter word.

Let's take a look at those situations from the check-in at the beginning of the book. Think about each one, and decide how you're going to use the power of no to get through each situation more successfully. Note down your ideas in the table below.

I can say no to an invitation when I don't want to go to an event.

··

I can say no to my boss when I need to.

··

I can say no to salespeople when I don't want to buy something.

··

I can say no to friends and family when they ask me for something I don't want to give.

because...

··

I can say no to my partner when I don't agree with them.

··

I can say no in a discussion without feeling afraid I'll start an argument.

··

I can say no when I want to stand up for what I believe in.

··

...and I'm going to use these techniques the next time this happens:

....

....

....

....

....

....

....

YOUR VERY OWN NO KIT

———

This book gives you lots of detailed information about all the different types of 'no' and how to use them, but if you're ever in a tight spot and need the power of no right now, this handy power-pack is here to help.

WHEN YOU NEED TO PREPARE YOURSELF

- Think about the possible outcomes and how you'll respond in each case.
- Remember that you deserve to be heard.
- Visualise the conversation going successfully and ending with a positive outcome.
- Take five deep breaths to calm yourself.
- Stand or sit in a power pose to make yourself feel strong.

WHEN YOU WANT TO GIVE A GENTLE NO

- Reassure the other person that they are important to you.
- Briefly explain the reason for your 'no'.
- Suggest an alternative solution.
- Empathise with the other person's situation.
- Keep the mood positive: your friendship is bigger than this one 'no'.
- *'I'm busy on Thursday, but I can help on Friday if you like?'*
- *'I can't come, but please let me know how it goes.'*
- *'Thank you for thinking of me, but I'm already committed this evening.'*

WHEN YOU NEED AN ASSERTIVE NO

- Stand or sit in a relaxed, open and upright position.
- Visualise what you want to achieve.
- State the facts of the situation and describe your desired outcome.
- Let go of the need to be liked and focus on your goals.
- *'I'd love to help, but my schedule's completely full until next week. Is that any good for you?'*
- *'I appreciate your asking me, but Anita is actually in charge of that account.'*
- *'I'll need to check my diary: let me get back to you on that.'*

WHEN IT'S TIME FOR A FIRM NO

- Remind yourself that you don't need to be everybody's friend.
- Repeat yourself if the other person won't listen to you.
- Don't feel obliged to give in if the other person keeps asking you.
- Remember that you have the right to say no to anything that makes you uncomfortable or unsafe.
- *'Thanks but this isn't for me.'*
- *'Sorry, I'm not interested.'*
- *'I can't help you with that.'*
- *'No.'*

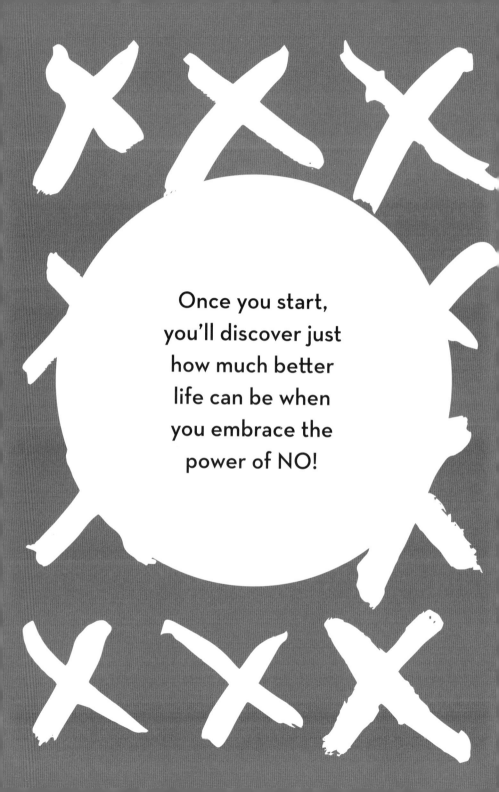

Once you start,
you'll discover just
how much better
life can be when
you embrace the
power of NO!

Acknowledgements

My thanks to all the people who helped make this book happen: Zara Anvari, Jenny Dye, Harriet Walker, Megan Brown, Roly Allen, Lucy Carter, Ben Gardiner and everyone else in the Octopus team; Pete Duncan, Laura Summers, Alison Jones, Jo West and all my other publishing friends; Mary, Mike and James Headon and the rest of my wonderful family; and last but not least Jeremy Catlin, who is himself a skilled practitioner of the power of no.

About the Author

Abbie Headon studied music at the University of Oxford and currently works as an editor and writer. She was included in *The Bookseller*'s list of Rising Stars 2018. Her books include *The Power of Yes, Poetry First Aid Kit* and *Literary First Aid Kit*, as well as titles on unicorns, grammar and seizing the day published under various pen names. She lives in Portsmouth. Say hello to Abbie on Twitter: @abbieheadon.